*to Haila Lawson Oct. 28, 2019
from Mom
Wm. Bradford,
10th Great Grandfather*

WITH GOD IN THE WILDERNESS

WILLIAM BRADFORD'S
HISTORY OF PLYMOUTH PLANTATION
RETOLD FOR YOUNG PEOPLE

MORE TITLES AVAILABLE FROM PSALM 78 MINISTRIES

Call Me No Hero

Daybreak in Alaska

Dangerous Endeavor: The Tale of the Lewis and Clark Expedition

Driven to Resistance: A History of the Revolutionary War, as told by those who lived it

Invisible Hero

I Want to Catch a Dinosaur

John Paton for Young Folks

My Life in Slavery

New Testament Greek for the Beginner

Pierre Viret: the Angel of the Reformation

Pirates, Puritans, and the Perils of the High Seas

Tremble: A Child's First Book on Space

Where is Wisdom? Where did God Hide It?

Without a Home or Country: A Stirring Tale of the Confederate Navy

Words of the Wise

For a full listing of titles, please visit: psalm78ministries.com

WITH GOD IN THE WILDERNESS

WILLIAM BRADFORD'S
HISTORY OF PLYMOUTH PLANTATION
RETOLD FOR YOUNG PEOPLE

William Bradford
R. A. Sheats

Psalm 78 Ministries

www.psalm78ministries.com

With God in the Wilderness: William Bradford's History of Plymouth Plantation retold for young people

by William Bradford and R. A. Sheats

Copyright © 2018 R. A. Sheats

All rights reserved.
No part of this publication may be reproduced or distributed in any form or by any means, without written consent from the publisher.

Published by:

Psalm 78 Ministries
P. O. Box 950
Monticello, FL 32345

www.psalm78ministries.com

ISBN: 978-1730756337

Printed in the United States of America.

TABLE OF CONTENTS

Introduction 9

1 Escape to Holland 11

2 Boarding the *Mayflower* 21

3 Onward to America! 27

4 Meeting the Savages 35

5 Attack! 41

6 A Terrible Winter 47

7 Planting the First Crop 57

8 Arrival of the *Fortune* 65

9 Squanto's Plot 71

10 Indian Conspiracy and Communism 80

11 Death of a Pastor 95

12 Friends from Leyden 101

13 A Murder Trial............................. 107

14 His Mercy Endures Forever 115

APPENDIX

Letter of Pastor John Robinson 127

"We could see nothing but a desolate wilderness, full of wild beasts and wild men. . . . What, then, could now sustain us but the Spirit of God and His grace?"

William Bradford, 1620

INTRODUCTION

After almost four hundred years, the exciting, inspiring, and remarkable history of Plymouth Plantation and the Pilgrims who established it is now available in an understandable, easy-to-read format, preserving this American classic for generations of young readers. Since its original publication in the 1600's, William Bradford's *Of Plymouth Plantation* has remained a classic text of American history, surviving almost four centuries of a nation's growth and change.

Persecution, arrest, secret escapes, perilous journeys across the ocean to a new and uncharted land, Indian attacks, jealousies, murders, conspiracy and intrigue fill the pages of Bradford's account of a small congregation of believers who desired nothing but a place to worship God according to the truths of Scripture. Through hardship and suffering, famine and want, freezing winters and scorching heat, Bradford captures the dangerous yet thrilling times in which he lived, and records for all posterity the faithful fulfillment of God's wondrous promise: "I will never leave you nor forsake you" (Heb. 13:5).

With God in the Wilderness offers the modern reader an understandable and comprehensible edition of Bradford's classic history. The text of this book has been taken from Harold Paget's 1920 edition. The work has been abridged and the English has been updated. Besides updating the English, one further change has been made to the manuscript. In Bradford's original work he referred to himself in the third person. This has been changed to the first person in order to make the story easier-to-understand for young people.

CHAPTER ONE

Escape to Holland

First I will unfold the causes that led to the foundation of the New Plymouth Settlement and the motives of those concerned in it. In order that I may give an accurate account of the project, I must begin at the very root and rise of it; and this I shall endeavor to do in a plain style and with particular regard to the truth—at least as near as my slender judgment can attain to it.

When England rejected Roman Catholicism and embraced the Reformation, two parties within the Church were formed. The one party of reformers attempted to establish the right worship of God and the discipline of Christ in the Church according to the simplicity of the gospel and without the mixture of men's inventions, and to be ruled by the laws of God's Word, according to the Scriptures. This group of believers was called *dissenters*. The other party—the episcopal—chose to cling to some forms of the Roman Catholic order of worship and church government.

The fight was so bitter between the two parties that neither the honor of God, the persecution to which both parties were subjected, nor the mediation of Mr. John Calvin and other worthy men, could prevail, and soon the church of dissenters was persecuted and accused of rebellion and high treason against the emperor and other such crimes.

The dissenters formed their own distinct bodies or churches and met separately. One of these churches was under the oversight of a man named John Robinson, who was

afterwards our pastor for many years, till the Lord took him away. Mr. William Brewster, a reverend man, was also chosen an elder of the church, and lived with us till old age.

However, the members of this church were not allowed to remain in England in peace. They were hunted and persecuted on every side. Some were clapped into prison; others had their houses watched night and day, and escaped with difficulty; and most were forced to flee and leave their homes and occupations. Yet, because these and many other even severer trials which afterwards befell them were only what they expected, they were able to bear them by the assistance of God's grace and spirit.

However, being thus troubled, and seeing that there was no hope of their remaining in England, they decided to flee into the Netherlands, where they heard there was freedom of religion for all. So, after about a year, having kept their meeting for the worship of God every Sabbath in one place or another despite the rage and malice of their adversaries, they resolved to get over to Holland as soon as they could—which was in the years 1607 and 1608.

For these reformers to be forced to leave their native soil, their lands and occupations, and all their friends, was a great sacrifice, and many people were astonished that they would abandon all this for the freedom to worship God. But these things did not dismay them (although they sometimes troubled them), for their desires were set on the ways of God. They rested on His providence, and knew whom they had believed (2 Tim. 1:12).

But, even though they could not remain in England, they were not allowed to leave. It was illegal for them to flee the country, so they had to seek secret ways of escape or bribe the captains of ships and pay exorbitant prices for their passages. Often they were betrayed and were placed in great danger.

A large number of them had decided to take passage from Boston in Lincolnshire, and for that purpose had hired a ship all to themselves and made agreement with the captain to be ready at a convenient place on a certain day to take them and their belongings aboard. After long waiting and great expense, the captain came at last and took them aboard at night. But, when he had secured them and their possessions, he betrayed them, having arranged beforehand with the searchers and other officers to do so. They then put them in open boats and there rifled and ransacked them, searching them to their shirts for money—and even the women, further than became modesty—and took them back to the town and made a spectacle of them to the multitude that came flocking on all sides to see them.

Being thus rifled and stripped of their money, books, and other property, they were brought before the magistrates, and messengers were sent to inform the lords of the Council about them. The magistrates treated them courteously and showed them what favor they could, but they dared not free them until order came from the council-table. The result was, however, that after a month's imprisonment the majority were freed and sent back to their homes, but seven of the leaders were kept in prison and were put on trial for their actions.

Next spring there was another attempt made by some of the same people, with others, to get over from a different place. They heard of a Dutchman at Hull who had a ship of his own, and they made an agreement with him and informed him of their troubles. They hoped he would be more trustworthy than the English captain had been, and he assured them that they needn't be afraid. He agreed to take them aboard between Grimsby and Hull, where there was a large area of open ground a far distance from any town.

The women and children, with all their possessions, were sent to the place in a small boat which they had hired, and the men were scheduled to meet them by land. But it so happened that they all arrived a day before the ship came. And, because the sea was rough and the women very sick, the sailors rowed into a creek nearby, where they became stuck at low water.

The next morning the ship came, but the little boat was stuck fast and could not move until about noon. In the meantime the captain of the ship, seeing how things were, sent his boat to get the men aboard whom he saw were ready and walking about the shore. But, after the first boatful was got aboard and she was ready to go for more, the captain saw a large body of horse and foot soldiers, armed with guns and other weapons—for the countryside had turned out to capture the fleeing families.

The Dutchman, seeing this, swore his country's oath, *"Sacramente!"* and, having a fair wind, weighed anchor, hoist sail, and sailed away! The poor men already aboard were in great distress for their wives and children who were left to be captured and were destitute of help. They feared for themselves, too, for they had nothing except the clothes on their backs, and scarcely a penny about them, for all their possessions were aboard the little boat which was now captured. It drew tears from their eyes, and they would have given anything to be ashore again. But it was all in vain; there was no remedy. And thus they were sadly parted.

Afterwards they endured a fearful storm at sea, and it was fourteen days or more before they reached port, in seven of which they saw neither sun, moon, nor stars, being driven near the coast of Norway. The sailors themselves often despaired, and once with shrieks and cries gave up all hope, as if the ship had foundered and they were sinking without hope of recovery. But, when man's hope and help wholly failed, then the Lord's power and mercy came to save them; for the ship rose again and gave the crew courage to manage her.

With fervent prayers the voyagers cried to the Lord in their great distress. They remained fairly composed and peaceful even when the water ran into their mouths and ears. And, when the sailors called out, "We sink, we sink!" they cried (if not with miraculous, yet with sublime faith): "Yet Lord, You can save; yet Lord, You can save!"

At this the ship not only righted herself, but shortly

afterwards the violence of the storm began to abate, and the Lord filled their afflicted minds with such comfort as but few can understand, and in the end brought them to their desired haven, where the people came flocking, astonished at their deliverance, for the storm had been so long and violent.

But to return to the rest where we left them. The other men, who were in greatest danger, made an attempt to escape before the troops could catch them, only remaining long enough to assist the women. But it was pitiful to see these poor women in their distress. What weeping and crying on every side! Some wept for their husbands carried away in the ship; others wept because they could not tell what would become of them and their little ones. Others also melted into tears when they saw their poor little ones hanging about them, crying for fear and shivering with cold!

Being thus captured by the soldiers, they were hurried from one place to another, till in the end the officers didn't know what to do with them. To imprison so many innocent women and children only because they wished to go with their husbands seemed unreasonable and would cause an outcry. But to send them home again was just as difficult, for the women confessed that they had no homes to go to—for they had sold their houses and possessions. To be short, after they had been thus troubled a good while and carried about from one constable to another, the magistrates were glad to be rid of them on any terms, for all were wearied and tired of them. Yet in the meantime they, poor souls, endured misery enough. So in the end necessity forced a way for them.

I must also mention, however, the fruit that came from all these troubles. For, by these public afflictions, the cause of this poor people became famous and led many to inquire into it. And their Christian behavior left a deep impression on the minds of many. Some people shrank from these first conflicts—and no wonder!—but many more came forward with fresh courage and inspired the rest. In the end, despite

the storms of opposition, they all got over to Holland, some from one place, some from another, and met together again with great rejoicing.

CHAPTER TWO

Boarding the *Mayflower*

After reaching the Netherlands, we struggled for several years to make a new home in this strange land. But, after we had lived here eleven or twelve years, our leaders began to fear the arrival of greater dangers and to consider a prudent way of escaping them. After we had spent much time considering and discussing the matter, we decided to seek a new location for a settlement. Many of our number were growing old and were unable to continue the life of hard labor necessary for their survival in the Netherlands. Their children also were suffering from the physical difficulties of the country.

But still more lamentable, and of all sorrows most heavy to be borne, was that many of the children, influenced by the difficulty of their present life, looked on the great godlessness of the young people of the country and the many temptations of the city and were led by evil example into dangerous paths. Casting off the reins of authority, they abandoned their parents. Some became soldiers, others embarked on voyages by sea, and others on worse courses tending to debauchery and the danger of their souls, to the great grief of their parents and the dishonor of God. So we saw that our posterity would be in danger of degenerating and becoming corrupt if we remained where we were.

Last and not least, we cherished a great hope and inward zeal of laying good foundations, or at least of making some way towards it, for the spread and advance of the gospel of the kingdom of Christ in the remote parts of the world, even if we only became stepping stones to others in the performance of

The *Mayflower*

so great a work.

These, and some other similar reasons, moved us to resolve to leave the Netherlands and journey to a new country. After much discussion it was decided to set our course for Virginia in the new continent of America.

Two of the men from our company journeyed to England and received permission to settle in the new land. The colony was financed by several merchants in London, among whom was a man named Mr. Thomas Weston. Mr. Weston promised his assistance to the company and helped to arrange matters for us in England.

Finally, after all had been prepared, we members of the church in the Netherlands who had decided to sail in the first trip to Virginia bought a ship and prepared to sail to England to meet the rest of our party. Another ship was hired at London, of about 180 tons, named the *Mayflower*.

When we were ready to depart, we held a day of solemn humiliation. Our pastor, Mr. Robinson, drew his sermon from Ezra 8:21: "And there at the river, by Ahava, I proclaimed a fast that we might humble ourselves before our God, and seek of Him a right way for us and for our children, and for all our substance." On this discourse he spent a good part of the day very profitably. The rest of the time was spent in pouring out prayers to the Lord with great fervency and abundance of tears. Mr. Robinson also sent a letter with us, by which he encouraged us to continue in repentance before God and brotherly love with one another.[1]

The time having come when we must depart, we were accompanied by most of our brethren out of the city to a town several miles off, called Delfthaven, where the ship lay ready to take us. So we left that good and pleasant city which had been our resting place for nearly twelve years. But we knew we were pilgrims, and lifted up our eyes to the heavens, our dearest country, and quieted our spirits.

When we came to the place, we found the ship and

---

[1] See the appendix of this book for Pastor Robinson's letter.

everything ready, and such of our friends as could not come with us followed us, and several came from Amsterdam to see us shipped and to take leave of us. That night there was little sleep for most of us, for it was spent in friendly fellowship and Christian conversation and other real expressions of true Christian love.

The next day the wind was fair, so we went aboard and our friends with us—and truly distressing was the sight of that sad and mournful parting. What sighs and sobs and prayers rose from among us! What tears gushed from every eye and tender speeches pierced each heart! Many of the Dutch strangers who stood on the quay as spectators could not refrain from tears. Yet it was comforting and sweet to see such lively and true expressions of dear and unfeigned love. But the tide which stays for no man called us away, though reluctant to part, and our reverent pastor, falling down on his knees, and all with him, with watery cheeks commended us with most fervent prayers to the Lord and His blessing. Then with mutual embraces and many tears we took our leave of one another—which proved to be the final parting for many of us.

Thus, hoisting sail, with a prosperous wind we came in a short time to Southampton, where we found the bigger ship from London lying ready with all the rest of the company. After concluding the rest of our business in London, we set sail from Southampton in the two ships about the 5th of August, 1620.

CHAPTER THREE

Onward to America!

Having put to sea, we had not gone far when Mr. Reynolds, the captain of the smaller ship, complained that he found her so leaky that he dare not go further till she was mended. So the captain of the bigger ship, Mr. Jones, was consulted, and they both resolved to put into Dartmouth and have her mended, which accordingly was done at great expense and loss of time and a fair wind. She was here thoroughly searched from stem to stern, some leaks were found and mended, and it was then believed that she might proceed without danger. So with good hope we put to sea again, thinking we would go comfortably on, not expecting any more hindrances of this kind.

But, after we had gone 100 leagues, the captain of the small ship again complained that she was so leaky that he must bear up or sink at sea, for they could scarcely keep her afloat by pumping. So they consulted again, and both ships resolved to bear up again and put into Plymouth, which accordingly was done. No special leak could be found, but it was judged to be the general weakness of the ship, and they feared that she would not prove equal to the voyage. At this we resolved to dismiss her, and part of the company, and proceed with the other ship. This, though it caused great discouragement, was done. So after we had taken out such provisions as the other ship could well stow, and decided what persons to send back, we made another sad parting, the one ship going back to London and the other proceeding on her voyage.

These troubles being over, and all being together in the one ship, we put to sea again on September 6th with a prosperous wind, which continued for several days and was some encouragement to us, though, as usual, many were afflicted with sea-sickness.

I must not omit to mention here a special example of God's providence. There was an insolent and very profane young man—one of the sailors, which made him the more overbearing—who was always harassing the poor people in their sickness and cursing them daily with grievous execrations. He didn't hesitate to tell them that he hoped to help throw half of them overboard before they came to their journey's end. If anyone gently reproved him, he would curse and swear most bitterly. But it pleased God, before they came halfway across the ocean, to smite the young man with a grievous disease, of which he died in a desperate manner, and so was himself the first to be thrown overboard. Thus his curses fell upon his own head, which astonished all his mates, for they saw that it was the just hand of God upon him.

After we had enjoyed fair winds and weather for some time, we encountered cross winds and many fierce storms by which the ship was much shaken and her upper works made very leaky. One of the main beams amid-ships was bent and cracked, which made us afraid that she might not be able to complete the voyage.

But, despite the danger, we committed ourselves to the will of God and resolved to proceed. In several of these storms the wind was so strong and the seas so high that we could not carry a knot of sail, but were forced to hull for many days. Once, as we thus lay at hull in a terrible storm, a strong young man, called John Rowland, coming on deck, was thrown into the sea. But it pleased God that he caught hold of the top-sail halyards which hung overboard and ran out at length. Even though he was several fathoms under water, he kept his hold until he was hauled up by the rope and then with a boat-hook helped into the ship and saved. And, though he was somewhat

Prayer aboard the *Mayflower*

ill from his adventure, he lived many years and became a profitable member both of the church and commonwealth. During the entire voyage only one of the passengers died.

Finally, after long beating at sea, on November 11th we caught sight of a part of the land called Cape Cod, at which we were not a little joyful. After some discussion among ourselves and with the captain, we tacked about and resolved to sail southward in an attempt to find some place near Hudson's River for our colony. But, after we had kept that course about half a day, we met with dangerous shoals and roaring breakers. And, since we knew we were in great danger, we decided to return to the Cape, and thought ourselves happy to get out of danger before night overtook us, as by God's providence we did. Next day we got into the bay, where we anchored in safety.

Having found a good haven and being brought safely in sight of land, we fell on our knees and blessed the God of Heaven who had brought us over the vast and furious ocean and delivered us from all the perils and miseries of it. How we rejoiced to again set our feet on the firm and stable earth, our proper element! And no marvel that we were thus joyful!

But here I must pause and stand half amazed at our poor people's present condition; and so I think will the reader, too, when he considers it well. Having thus passed the vast ocean, and that sea of troubles before while we were making our preparations, we now had no friends to welcome us, no inns to entertain and refresh our weather-beaten bodies, and no houses—much less towns—to go to.

It is recorded in Scripture, as a mercy to the apostle Paul and his shipwrecked crew, that the barbarians showed them no small kindness in refreshing them. But these savage barbarians, when we met with them, were readier to fill our sides full of arrows than otherwise! As for the season, it was winter, and those who have experienced the winters of the country know them to be sharp and severe and subject to fierce storms, when it is dangerous to travel to known places—much more to search an unknown coast. Besides, what could we see but a desolate wilderness, full of wild beasts and wild men; and how many of them there might be we knew not! Neither could we, as it were, go up to the top of Pisgah, to view from this wilderness a more goodly country to encourage our hopes. For, no matter which way we turned (except upward to Heaven!), our eyes could catch very little hope from any outward objects. Since summer was passed, all things turned upon us a weather-beaten face. And the whole country, full of woods and thickets, presented a wild and savage view.

If we looked behind us, there was the mighty ocean which we had crossed over, and was now a gulf separating us from all civilized parts of the world. Indeed, we had very little hope of further assistance from England, and thus had little to support our courage in this sad condition and the trials we were under. It's true, indeed, that the affection and love of our brethren at Leyden towards us was cordial and unbroken, but they had little power to help us or themselves.

What, then, could now sustain us but the Spirit of God and His grace? Ought not the children of their fathers rightly to say: "Our fathers were Englishmen who came over the great ocean, and were ready to perish in this wilderness; but they cried unto the Lord, and He heard their voice, and looked on their adversity. Let them therefore praise the Lord, because He is good, and His mercies endure forever. Yea, let them that have been redeemed of the Lord, show how He hath delivered them from the hand of the oppressor. When they wandered forth into the desert-wilderness, out of the way, and found no city to dwell in, both hungry and thirsty, their soul was overwhelmed in them. Let them confess before the Lord His lovingkindness, and His wonderful works before the sons of men!" (*see* Deut. 26:5-10; Psa. 107:1-8.)

CHAPTER FOUR

Meeting the Savages

Thus we arrived at Cape Cod on the 11th of November, 1620, and necessity called on us to look out for a place of habitation. Having brought a large shallop (a small ship) with us from England, we now got her out and set our carpenters to work to trim her up. But, because she was much bruised and battered in the foul weather at sea, we saw that it would take a great deal of time to repair her. So a few of the men volunteered to go by land and explore the countryside while the shallop was put in order—particularly since, when they entered the bay, there seemed to be an opening some two or three leagues off, which the captain thought was a river.

We thought that there might be some danger in this attempt. But, since the men were determined to go, sixteen of them, well-armed, were permitted to leave under the command of Captain Miles Standish. They set forth on the 15th of November.

When the men had marched about a mile by the seashore, they spied five or six persons with a dog coming towards them. They were savages, but they fled back into the woods, followed by the English, who wanted to speak with them and discover whether there were any more lying in ambush. But the Indians, seeing themselves followed, left the woods and ran along the sands as hard as they could, so our men could not catch up with them, but followed the track of their feet several miles. However, when night came on, they stopped and made camp. Then, after setting sentinels, they rested in peace.

Next morning the men again pursued the Indians' tracks until they came to a wide creek where the savages had left the shore and turned into the woods. They continued to follow them by guess, hoping to find their dwellings. But soon they lost both the Indians and themselves, and fell into such thickets that their clothes and armor were injured severely, though they suffered most from lack of water. At length they found some, and refreshed themselves with the first New England water they had drunk. And in their great thirst they found it as pleasant as wine or beer had been before.

Afterwards they directed their course towards the other shore, for they knew it was only a neck of land they had to cross over. At length they got to the seashore and marched to this supposed river, and by the way found a pond of fresh water, and shortly after a quantity of cleared ground where the Indians had formerly planted corn. They also found some of their graves.

Proceeding further, they saw stubble where corn had been grown the same year, and also found a place where a house had lately been, with some planks and a great kettle and heaps of sand newly-banked, under which they found several large baskets filled with corn, some in the ear of various colors, which was a very surprising sight, for they had never seen anything like it before. This was near the supposed river that they had come to seek.

When they reached the river, they found that it opened into two arms, with a high cliff of sand at the entrance, but more likely to be creeks of salt water than fresh, they thought. There was good harborage for their shallop, so they left it to be further explored when she was ready. The time allowed them having expired, they returned to the ship, lest the others should be anxious about their safety. They took part of the corn and buried the rest. And so, like the men from Eschol, they carried with them of the fruits of the land, and showed their brethren, at which the rest were very glad and greatly encouraged.

Finding the corn

After this, when the shallop was ready, they set out again to explore the area. The captain of the ship wanted to go himself, so there were some thirty men in the party. However, they found it to be no harbor for ships, but only for boats. They also found two of the Indians' houses covered with mats, and some of their implements in them; but the people had run away and could not be seen.

They also found more corn, and beans of various colors. These they took with them, and intended to pay for them when they met with the savages (which they were able to do about six months later). And I must note this as a special providence of God and a great mercy to our poor people, for in this way we got seed to plant corn the next year, or else we might have starved, for we had none—nor any chance of getting any—until it would have been too late for the planting season. But the Lord never forsakes His own in their great need. Let His holy name have all the praise!

CHAPTER FIVE

Attack!

We spent the month of November exploring, until foul weather put an end to our attempts. Then, on the 6th of December, we sent out our shallop again with ten of our main men and some sailors to explore further and look for a suitable place to establish our colony. The weather was very cold, and it froze so hard that the spray of the sea froze on their coats like glass. Early that night the men reached the lower end of the bay. And, as they drew near the shore, they saw ten or twelve Indians very busy about something. They landed about a league or two from them, but it was late when they landed, so they made themselves a barricade of logs and branches as well as they could in the time, and set up a guard. Then the rest of them went to sleep. In the distance they could see the smoke of the fire that the savages made that night.

When morning came the men divided their party and sent some to coast along the shore in the boat and the rest to march through the woods to explore the land and, if possible, find a suitable place for our settlement.

They wandered up and down all that day, but found no people or any place they liked. When the sun got low, they hastened out of the woods to meet their shallop, making signs to it to come into a creek nearby, which it did at high water. They were very glad to meet, for they had not seen each other since the morning. They then made a barricade (as they did every night) with logs, stakes, and thick pine branches, the height of a man, leaving it open to leeward, partly to shelter them from the cold wind and partly to defend them from any sudden attacks of the savages in case they attempted to surround them.

Making their fire in the middle of their encampment and lying around it, the men quickly fell asleep, being very weary. But about midnight they heard a hideous cry and their sentinel called "Arm, arm!" So they leapt up and took hold of their weapons and shot a couple of muskets. Then the noise ceased. They decided that it was a pack of wolves or some wild beasts, for one of the sailors told them that he had often heard such noises in Newfoundland. So they rested till about five o'clock in the morning.

After prayer they prepared for breakfast. And, since the day was dawning, they decided it was time to begin carrying things down to the boat. Some of the men said that they shouldn't carry their guns down, but others said that they would be more prepared if they did. But three or four of the men refused to carry their guns down to the boat until they went down themselves.

However, since the water wasn't high enough, the other men laid their guns down on the bank of the creek and came back up to breakfast.

But soon, all of a sudden, they heard a loud and strange cry, which they recognized as the same that they had heard in the night. One of the company who was outside came running in and cried: "Men—Indians, Indians!" and at the same moment their arrows came flying among them!

Some of the men ran down to the creek as quickly as they could to recover their guns, which (by the providence of God) they succeeded in doing. In the meantime two of those who were still armed fired their muskets at the Indians and two more stood ready at the entrance of their encampment, but were commanded not to shoot until they could be certain of their aim. The other two men loaded again at full speed, for there were only four guns there to defend the barricade when it was first attacked.

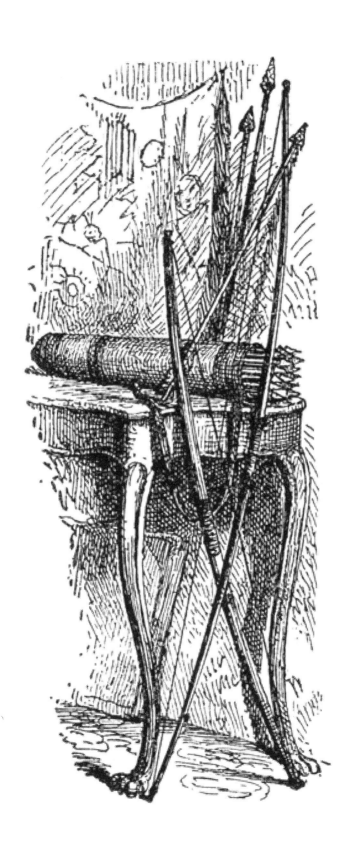

The cry of the Indians was dreadful, especially when they saw the men run out of the barricade towards the shallop to recover their guns. The Indians swarmed around them, but some of the men, armed with coats of mail and with cutlasses in their hands, soon got their guns and fired them among them, which quickly stopped their violence. There was one big Indian, and no less valiant, who stood behind a tree within half a musket-shot, and let his arrows fly at them. He was seen to shoot three arrows, which were all avoided. He stood three musket-shots, till one of them made the bark and splinters of the tree fly about his ears, at which he gave an extraordinary shriek, and away all of them went.

The men then left some of the party to guard the shallop and followed the Indians about a quarter of a mile, shouting once or twice and shooting off two or three guns, and then returned. They did this so that the natives wouldn't think they were afraid of them.

Thus it pleased God to vanquish their enemies and give them deliverance. And by His special providence He so protected them that not one of them was hit, even though the arrows came close to them on every side and some of their coats which were hung up in the barricade were shot through and through. Afterwards they gave God solemn thanks and praise for their deliverance, and gathered up a bundle of the arrows, and later sent them to England by the captain of the ship. They called the place "The First Encounter."

Then they left, and before long discovered a suitable place for the colony. They returned to the ship, and on the 15th of December the ship weighed anchor to go to the place they had discovered. On the 25th of that month we began to erect the first house for common use to receive us and our goods.

CHAPTER SIX

A Terrible Winter

Before I continue, I must turn back a little and explain that we drew up a compact or deed before we went ashore to establish ourselves, which was the first foundation of our government. We did this because some of the strangers among us said that they wouldn't abide by any rules because we weren't settling in Virginia as we had thought, but were instead settling much further north. Therefore we drew up a compact in these words:

> In the name of God, Amen.
> We whose names are underwritten, the loyal subjects of our dread sovereign lord, King James, by the grace of God, of Great Britain, France and Ireland, King, Defender of the Faith, etc., having undertaken for the glory of God, and advancement of the Christian faith, and honor of our king and country, a voyage to plant the first colony in the northern parts of Virginia, do by these presents solemnly and mutually in the presence of God, and of one another, covenant and combine ourselves into a civil body politic, for our better ordering and preservation, and the furtherance of the ends aforesaid and by virtue hereof to enact, constitute, and frame, such just and equal laws, ordinances, acts, constitutions, and offices, from time to time, as shall be thought most meet and convenient for the general use of the Colony, unto which we promise all due submission and obedience. In witness whereof we have here underscribed our names at

Cape Cod, 11th of November, in the year of the reign of our sovereign lord, King James of England, France and Ireland the eighteenth, and of Scotland the fifty-fourth. A.D. 1620.

Then we chose, or rather confirmed, Mr. John Carver, a godly man and highly approved among us, as our governor for that year. Then we built a place for our goods and common stores, which took us a long time to unload because we lacked sufficient boats and because the weather was so severe and many among us were sick. While we did this and began erecting cottages to live in, we met to discuss the formation of our civil and military government to better establish law and order.

But soon a most lamentable blow fell upon us. In two or three months' time half of our company died, partly owing to the severity of the winter (especially during January and February) and the lack of houses and other comforts, and partly to scurvy and other diseases which our long voyage and our uncomfortable quarters had brought upon us. Of the more than one hundred persons, scarcely fifty survived, and sometimes two or three persons died in a single day.

In the time of worst distress, there were only six or seven healthy persons who, to their great commendation, spared no pains night or day, but with great toil and at the risk of their own health fetched wood, made fires, prepared food for the sick, made their beds, washed their infected clothes, dressed and undressed them—in a word they did all the homely and necessary services for them which dainty and queasy stomachs cannot endure to hear mentioned—and all this they did willingly and cheerfully, without the least complaining, and thus revealed their love to the friends and brethren. This is a rare example, and worthy to be remembered.

Two of these seven were Mr. William Brewster, our reverend elder, and Miles Standish, our captain and military commander, to whom myself and many others were much

Captain Miles Standish

beholden in our low and sick condition. And yet the Lord so upheld these men that in this general calamity they were not at all infected with sickness. And what I have said of these few I should say of many others who died in this general visitation, and others yet living, that while they had health or strength, they forsook none that had need of them. I doubt not that their recompense is with the Lord.

But I must not pass by another remarkable and unforgettable occurrence. When this calamity fell among the passengers who were to be left here to settle, the sailors hurried them ashore and made them drink water so that the sailors could have more beer. And, when one sufferer in his sickness requested only a small can of beer, they told him that even if he were their own father they wouldn't give him any.

Then the disease began to seize the sailors also, so that almost half of the crew died before they went away, including many of their officers and strongest men, among them the boatswain, gunner, three quarter-masters, the cook, and others. At this the captain was somewhat struck, and sent to the sick ashore and told the governor that he could send for beer for those who had need of it, even if he had to drink water on the homeward voyage.

Throughout this time the Indians came skulking about those who were ashore and would sometimes show themselves afar off, at a distance. But, when anyone approached them, they would run away. Once they stole away the men's tools where they had been working and had gone to dinner.

About the 16th of March a certain Indian came boldly among us and spoke to us in broken English, which we could easily understand but were astonished to hear. At last we understood by speaking with him that he was not from these parts but belonged to the eastern country where some English ships came to fish. And with some of these English he was acquainted, and could name several of them. From them he had obtained his knowledge of the language. He became useful to us in acquainting us with many things concerning the state of the country in the east parts where he lived. His name was Samoset.

Samoset also told us about another Indian whose name was Squanto. He was a native of this part who had been in England and could speak English better than himself. After we entertained him hospitably for some time and sent him away with gifts, he returned in a little while with five more Indians, and they brought back all the tools that had been stolen. They also prepared for the coming of their great Sachem or chief, called Massasoit, who came about four or five days later with the chief of his friends and other attendants, and with Squanto. With him, after friendly entertainment and some gifts, we made a peace treaty which has now continued for twenty-four years.

These were the terms of peace:

1. That neither he nor any of his should injure or harm any of our people.
2. That if any of his did any harm to any of ours, he would send the offender to us so that we might punish him.
3. That if anything were taken away from any of ours, he would cause it to be restored; and we would do the same to his.
4. If any made unjust war against him, we would aid him. If any made war against us, he would aid us.
5. He would send to his neighboring confederates and inform them of this peace, so that they might not wrong us, but might also be included in the conditions of peace.
6. That when their men came to us, they would leave their bows and arrows behind them.

After this he returned to his place, called Sowams (about forty miles off), but Squanto stayed with us and served as our interpreter, and became a special instrument sent by God for our good, beyond our wildest expectations. He showed us how to plant their corn, where to catch fish and other commodities, and guided us to unknown places, and never left us till he died.

Signing the Peace Treaty

Meeting Massasoit

Squanto was a native of these parts and had been one of the few survivors of the plague that passed through here shortly before the English arrived. He was carried away with others by a man by the name of Hunt, a captain of a ship, who intended to sell them for slaves in Spain. But Squanto escaped and went to England. He was received by a merchant in London and employed in Newfoundland and other parts, and lastly brought into these parts by a Captain Dermer.

But to return. When spring arrived it pleased God to cause the mortality to begin to cease among us, and the sick recovered quickly, which put new life into us all—though the people had borne their sad afflictions with as much patience and contentment as I think any people could do. But it was the Lord who upheld us and who had prepared us beforehand, for many had long borne the yoke—indeed, even from their youth.

Squanto teaches how to plant corn

CHAPTER SEVEN

Planting the First Crop

We now decided to send back the ship which had brought us over and which had remained till about this time or the beginning of April, 1621. The reason, on our part, why she had stayed so long, was the necessity and danger we were in. It was well towards the end of December before she could land anything or we were in a condition to receive anything ashore. And after that, on the 14th of January, the house we had built for a general rendezvous accidentally caught fire, and some of us had to go aboard the ship for shelter.

Then the sickness began to fall among us with severity. Also the governor and the chief members of the people, seeing so many fall sick and die daily, thought it unwise to send the ship away, considering their condition and the danger we were in from the Indians, till we could obtain some shelter. We therefore thought it better to incur further expense for ourselves and our friends than to risk everything. The captain also had many of the crew sick and dying, and did not dare put to sea until they began to recover and until the heart of winter was over.

The settlers, as many as were able, then began to plant our corn, in which service Squanto helped us greatly by showing us how to plant it and cultivate it. He also told us that unless we got fish to fertilize the exhausted old soil, it would come to nothing. He showed us that in the middle of April plenty of fish would come up the brook beside which we had begun to build, and taught us how to catch them and where to get other necessary provisions. We also planted some English seed, such as wheat and peas, but it came to no good either because of the badness of the seed or the lateness of the season or some other defect.

We worked the fields together in a form of communal service (known as communism), and hoped to provide for the colony in this way. Each man worked as he was able, and we divided the harvest equally between us.

This April, while we were busy sowing our seed, our governor, Mr. John Carver, one hot day came out of the field very sick. He complained greatly of his head and lay down, and within a few hours his senses failed. He never spoke again and died a few days later. His death was greatly mourned, and depressed us deeply, with good reason. He was buried in the best manner possible, with some volleys of shot fired by all those who bore arms. His wife, a frail woman, died five or six weeks after him.

Shortly after this, I, William Bradford, was chosen governor in his place. But I had not yet recovered from my illness, in which I had lain near the point of death. Therefore Isaac Allerton was appointed as my assistant. The two of us, by renewed elections each year, continued several years together in these offices.

On May 12th the first marriage here took place, which we thought proper for the magistrate to perform since it is a civil institution upon which many questions about inheritance depend, and other things requiring their recognition. We also did this because it agrees with the Scriptures (Ruth 4), and because marriage is never mentioned in the gospels as a part of the minister's duty.

Having now made some progress with our affairs at home, we thought it advisable to send a deputation to our new friend Massasoit and to bestow on him some gift to bind him faster to us. We also did this so that we could view the country and see how he lived, what strength he had about him, and where his dwelling place was located in case we ever needed

The first marriage in Plymouth

to reach him.

So on July 2nd we sent Mr. Edward Winslow and Mr. Hopkins, with Squanto as their guide. They gave Massasoit a suit of clothes and a horseman's coat, with some other small things which were kindly accepted, though our men weren't fed well, and came home both weary and hungry. The Indians in those times did not have nearly as much corn as they have had since the English supplied them with hoes and set an example by their industry in preparing new ground with them.

Massasoit's place was found to be forty miles off in an area with good soil. But his people had died in great numbers during the recent plague throughout these parts (about three years before the coming of the English). Thousands of them died, until the living weren't able to bury the dead, and their skulls and bones were found in many places lying still above ground where their houses and dwelling places had been—a very sad sight. But they brought word that the Narragansetts lived just on the other side of the great bay and were a strong, populous tribe living close together, and had not been attacked by this deadly plague.

About the end of this month John Billington lost himself in the woods and wandered up and down for about five days, living on berries and whatever he could find. At last he came across an Indian plantation twenty miles to the south called Manamet. They carried him further off to Nauset, among the Indians who had attacked the landing party when they were coasting and while our ship lay at the Cape, as I mentioned earlier. But I inquired after him among the Indians, and at length Massasoit sent us word where he was, and I sent a shallop for him and rescued him. The Indians there also came and made their peace, and full payment was given by the settlers to those whose corn they had found and taken when we were at Cape Cod.

Thus our peace and acquaintance was pretty well established with the natives around us.

After this, on the 18th of September, we sent out our shallop with ten men and Squanto as guide and interpreter to the Massachusetts tribe, to explore the bay and trade with the natives, which we accomplished and were kindly received. The Indians were much afraid of the Tarantines, a tribe to the eastward, who used to come at harvest time and take away their corn and often kill some of them. Our men returned in safety and brought home a good quantity of beaver skins. And thus we found the Lord to be with us in all our ways, and to bless our outgoings and incomings, for which let His holy name have the praise forever, to all posterity.

We began now to gather in the small harvest we had and to prepare our houses for the winter. By this time we had recovered in health and strength and were plentifully provisioned, for while some had been thus employed in affairs away from home, others were occupied in fishing for cod, bass, and other fish, of which they caught a good quantity, every family having their portion. All the summer there was no lack.

And now, as winter approached, wild fowl began to arrive, of which there were plenty when they came here first, though afterwards they became scarcer. As well as wild fowl, we got an abundance of wild turkeys, besides venison, etc. Each person had about a peck of meal a week, or now, since harvest, Indian corn in that proportion. Afterwards many wrote at length about their plenty to their friends in England—not false but true reports.

CHAPTER EIGHT

Arrival of the *Fortune*

In November, about twelve months after our arrival, a small ship came unexpectedly, bringing Mr. Cushman and with him thirty-five persons to remain and live in the plantation; at which we rejoiced greatly. And the new arrivals, when they came ashore and found all well and saw plenty of victuals in every house, were no less glad. Most of them were healthy young men, though many of them were wild enough, who had little considered what they were undertaking until they reached the harbor of Cape Cod.

So they were all landed, but they didn't even bring flour or any other supplies with them, or any bedding except some poor things they had in their cabins, or any pots or pans to cook any food in, or many clothes, for many of them had sold their coats and cloaks when they left England. But some suits of clothes had been sent over in the ship, out of which they were supplied. The plantation was glad of this addition of strength, but could have wished that many of them had been of better class and all of them better furnished with provisions, but that could not now be helped.

This ship, called the *Fortune*, was quickly sent away after being loaded with good clapboard, as full as she could stow, and two hogsheads of beaver and otter skins, which we had traded in exchange for a few trifling commodities we brought with us at first. The cargo was estimated to be worth nearly £500. Mr. Cushman returned with the ship, as Mr. Weston and the rest had commissioned him, so that he could

inform the partners in England how matters stood in the New World.

Mr. Weston, who was arranging matters in England, sent a letter promising to supply us with all we needed. We therefore hoped to receive supplies before much time had passed, but things turned out otherwise, for Mr. Weston quickly abandoned us. So vain is confidence in man!

After the departure of this ship, which did not stay more than fourteen days, I and my assistant settled the new arrivals with several families as best as we could, and took an exact account of all our provisions in store, and proportioned the same to the number of persons, and found that it would not hold out above six months at half allowance, and hardly that. We could not well give less this winter, till fish came in again. So we were all quickly put on half rations, one as well as another. It became irksome, but we bore it patiently, hoping to receive fresh supplies soon.

Soon after the ship's departure, the great Narragansett tribe, in a boastful way, sent a messenger to us with a bundle of arrows tied up with a large snake skin. Our interpreters told us that this was a threatening challenge. At this the governor (myself), with the advice of the others, sent the Narragansetts a reply, stating that if they would rather have war than peace, they could begin when they wished. We told them that we had done them no wrong and we didn't fear them, nor would they find us unprepared. We sent the snakeskin back by another messenger with bullets in it, but the Indians would not accept it and returned it again. The Narragansetts probably did this out of prideful ambition, thinking that, since so many of the surrounding Indians had died in the recent plague, they could rule over the rest of them, and that the English would be a hindrance to their plans since Massasoit had already taken shelter under our wings.

But this made us much more careful to stand guard and beware. We agreed to surround our dwellings with a good strong stockade and make flankers in convenient places, with gates to shut. These gates we locked every night and set a watch. And, when need required, we also set up outposts in the daytime. The colonists, at the captain's and governor's advice, were divided into four squadrons, and every one had his appointed place, to which he should go at any sudden alarm.

Loading the *Fortune* with clapboard

Building the stockade

And, in case of fire, a company with muskets was appointed as a guard to prevent Indian treachery while the others put out the fire. This was accomplished very cheerfully, and the town was enclosed by the beginning of March, every family having a pretty garden plot.

CHAPTER NINE

Squanto's Plot

We had arranged with the Massachusetts Indians to go again and trade with them in the spring, and began to prepare for the voyage about the latter end of March, 1622. But Hobbamok, our Indian friend, told us that, from some rumors he had heard, he feared they had joined the Narragansetts and might betray us if we weren't careful. He also hinted that he suspected Squanto of something because he had seen him whispering privately with some of the other Indians. But we decided to proceed anyway, and sent out our shallop with ten of their chief men about the beginning of April.

The men brought both Squanto and Hobbamok with them, considering the jealousy between them. But they had not been gone long from the settlement before an Indian belonging to Squanto's family came running in, apparently in great fear, and told them that many of the Narragansetts with Corbitant (and he thought also with Massasoit), were coming to attack us. He said that he had come away to warn us even though he endangered himself by coming.

Being questioned by me, he acted as if the enemy were at hand, and kept looking back as if they were at his heels. At this I ordered the settlers to take arms and stand on their guard. And, thinking the boat would still be within hearing since it was a calm day, I ordered a warning piece or two to be shot off, which they heard and returned. But no Indians appeared. And, though watch was kept all night, nothing was seen.

Hobbamok was confident of Massasoit's good faith and thought the rumor was all false. But I had Hobbamok send his wife privately to see what she could observe, on pretence of other purposes, but nothing was found and all was quiet. So they proceeded on their voyage to the Massachusetts and had good trade and returned in safety—blessed be God!

But by what had happened we began to see that Squanto sought his own ends and played his own game by frightening the Indians and getting gifts from them for himself, making them believe that he could stir up war against them if he wanted to, and make peace for whoever he wanted. He even made them believe that the English kept the plague buried in the ground and could send it among them whenever they wished, which terrified the Indians and made them more dependent on him than on Massasoit. This made him envied, and was likely to have cost him his life. For, after discovering this, Massasoit sought both privately and openly to have him killed. This caused Squanto to stick close to the English, and he never dared leave us till he died.

The colony also made good use of the jealousy between Hobbamok and him, which made them both behave more honestly, for I pretended to favor the one and Captain Standish the other, by which we obtained better information and made them both more zealous in our service.

Now our provisions were practically all exhausted and we looked anxiously for supplies, but none came. About the latter end of May, however, we spied a boat at sea which at first we thought was some Frenchman, but it proved to be a shallop which came from a ship which Mr. Weston and another man had sent out fishing at a place called Damariscove, forty leagues to the eastward of us, where that year many ships had come to fish. This boat brought seven passengers and some letters, but no provisions and no hope of any. Mr. Weston instead sent out these men to plant a rival colony in Massachusetts and sent us no aid.

Thus all our hopes in regard to Mr. Weston were laid in

"We built a fort with good timber."

the dust, and all his promised help turned into empty words. And we were thus not only left destitute of help in our extreme want, having neither food nor anything to trade with, but were discouraged to see that Mr. Weston hoped to obtain a fortune through his own attempts at fishing and trading instead of assisting us. And thus others were preparing to gather up what the country might have provided for our relief.

In these dire straits, deserted by those from whom we had hoped to obtain supplies, and famine beginning to pinch us severely, the Lord, who never fails His own, provided assistance beyond all expectation. A boat which came from the eastward brought us a letter from a stranger whose name we had never even heard before, the captain of a fishing ship. This captain brought us news about an Indian massacre at Jamestown and warned us to be on our guard against the savages in our area. He also offered to supply us with provisions if we had need. We sent Mr. Winslow to trade with him, who obtained a good quantity of provisions and returned in safety. Thus the plantation had a double benefit: first, they were refreshed at the time by the food obtained; secondly, they realized that they had neighbors to whom they could appeal in future in time of need.

What this small boat brought, divided among so many, came to very little. Yet still, by God's blessing, it sustained us until harvest. It amounted to a quarter of a pound of bread a day for each person. This I distributed daily. If I had given it all to the people at once, they would have eaten it up and then starved. In this way, with what else we could obtain, we survived until our corn was ripe.

This summer we built a fort with good timber—a handsome building and a good defense, made with a flat roof and battlement, on which our ordnance was mounted, and where we kept constant watch, especially in time of danger. It also served as a meeting house and was fitted accordingly for that use. It was a big undertaking for us at this period of weakness and want, but the dangerous times necessitated it.

And the continual rumors about the Indians here, especially the Narragansetts, and also the news of the great massacre in Virginia, made all hands willing to complete it.

Now the welcome time of harvest approached, in which we all had our hungry bellies filled. But it amounted to but little compared with a full year's supply, partly because we were not yet used to the culture of Indian corn and partly owing to our many other employments. But it was mainly our weakness because of lack of food which prevented us from cultivating the crops as we should have done.

Shortly after harvest Mr. Weston's people, who were now settled in Massachusetts and who had, by disorder as it seems, made havoc of their provisions, began now to realize that famine would come to them. Finding that the people here had bought trading commodities and intended to trade for corn, they wrote to me and asked to be permitted to join us in trading, and offered the use of their small ship for the purpose. They also asked us to either lend or to sell them some of our trading commodities in return, and promised to pay for them when Mr. Weston or their supplies arrived.

I, as governor, agreed to do so on equal terms, intending to go round the cape southwards with the ship, where corn could be obtained. Captain Standish was appointed to go with them, and Squanto as a guide and interpreter, about the end of September. But the winds soon drove them in and, when they set out again, Captain Standish fell ill with fever, so I went myself instead. But we could not get round the shoals of Cape Cod because of the flats and breakers, and Squanto could not direct us to a better route.

The captain of the boat dared not venture any further, so we put into Manamoick Bay and got what we could there.

Here Squanto fell ill of Indian fever, bleeding much at the nose—which the Indians take for a symptom of death—and within a few days he died. He begged the governor to pray for him so that he might go to the Englishmen's God in heaven. He also bequeathed several of his things to some of his English

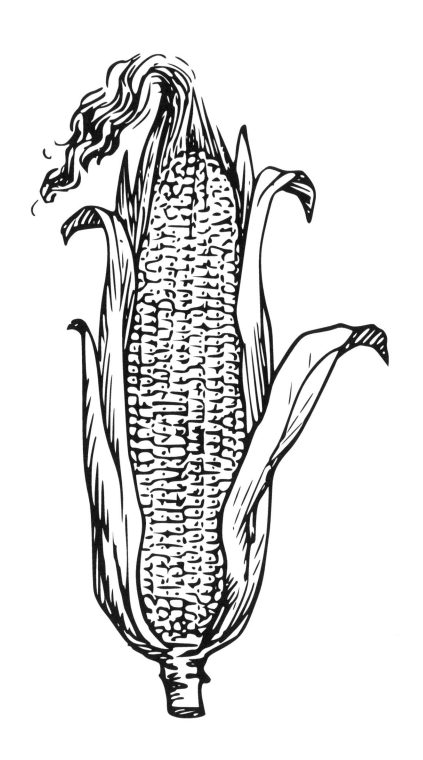

friends, as remembrances. His death was a great loss.

On this voyage we got in one place or another about 26 or 28 hogsheads of corn and beans, which was more than the Indians could well spare hereabouts, for they planted but little till they got English hoes. So we had to return, disappointed that we could not get round the Cape and were not better laden. Afterwards I took a few men and went to inland places to get what I could, to be fetched home in the spring, which was some help.

CHAPTER TEN

Indian Conspiracy and Communism

Because the Weston colony fell into such extremity, they began to sell their clothes and bed-coverings. Some among them even became servants to the Indians, cutting them wood and fetching them water for a capful of corn. Others began stealing from the Indians, of which they complained bitterly. In the end some starved and died from cold and hunger. At last most of them left their dwellings and scattered up and down in the woods and by the water-side, a few here and a few there, wherever they could find ground-nuts and clams.

The Indians treated them with contempt because of their actions and circumstances, and began to insult them in a most insolent manner. Often, while they were cooking a pot of ground-nuts or shellfish, when it was ready, the Indians would come and eat it up. And at night they would come and steal the blankets from the few men who had any left, and let them lie in the cold. Their condition was very pitiable, and in the end, in order to satisfy the Indians, they were obliged to hang one of their own men whom they could not keep from stealing.

While things went on thus, I and the people here learned that our friend Massasoit was sick, and near to death. We visited him, and brought whatever we could to relieve him, and he recovered. He then revealed to us a conspiracy

Visiting Massasoit

among the Indians of Massachusetts and other neighboring tribes, who had conspired to wipe out Mr. Weston's people in revenge for the continual injuries they did them, and who planned to take opportunity of their weakness to do it. And, believing that the people at New Plymouth would avenge their death, the Indians had decided to do the same to us, and had asked Massasoit to join them. He advised us to prevent it by speedily capturing some of the chief of the conspirators before it was too late.

This news troubled us greatly, and we took it into serious consideration. And, after a full investigation, we found other evidence too lengthy to describe that proved the truth of Massasoit's words.

In the meantime one of Mr. Weston's people came from Massachusetts with a small pack on his back. And, though he did not know a foot of the way, he got here safely. He lost his way, which was well for him. For, though he was pursued by the Indians, they didn't catch him because he got lost and took a different path than they expected. He told us how everything stood among them and explained that he dared not stay there any longer. He believed, by what he saw, that the Indians would murder them all shortly.

So the people at New Plymouth acted quickly and sent a boat with Captain Standish and some men, who found Mr. Weston's men in a miserable condition, out of which he rescued them, and killed a few of the chief conspirators among the Indians. Then, according to his orders, he offered to bring the remnant of the Weston settlement here if they desired it, in which case they would be supplied as well as the colonists here until Mr. Weston or some supplies came to them. Or, if they preferred any other course, he was to give them any assistance he could.

They thanked him, but most of them begged him to give them some corn so that they could go with their small ship to the eastward, where they hoped to hear news of Mr. Weston or get some supplies from him since it was the time of the year

for the fishing ships to be out. If they couldn't obtain any news or supplies, they planned to work among the fishermen for their living and get their passage back to England if they heard nothing from Mr. Weston in the meantime. So he put aboard what they had, and he got them all the corn he could spare, scarcely leaving enough to bring himself home, and saw them well out of the bay, under sail at sea. Then he came back, not accepting a pennyworth of anything from them.

This was the end of those who at one time boasted of their strength—all able, healthy men—and what they would do in comparison with the people here, who had many women and children and weak ones among them. But a man's way is not in his own hands. God can make the weak to stand. Let him also that stands take heed lest he fall.

Shortly after, when he heard of the ruin and destitution of his colony, Mr. Weston came over with some of the fishermen, under another name and disguised as a blacksmith. He got a boat and with a man or two came to see how things were there. But on the way ashore he was caught in a storm, his shallop was sunk in the bay, and he barely escaped with his life.

Afterwards he fell into the hands of the Indians, who robbed him of all that he had saved from the wreck, and stripped him of all his clothes to his shirt. At last he got to Piscataqua and borrowed a suit of clothes, and so came to New Plymouth. This was a strange alteration in him for those who had seen him in his former flourishing condition. So uncertain are the mutable things of this unstable world! And yet men set their hearts upon them, though they daily see their vanity.

All this while no supplies were heard of, nor did we know when we might expect any. So we began to consider how to raise more corn and obtain a better crop than we had done, so that we might not continue to endure the misery of want. At length, after much debate, the governor, with the advice of the main men among them, allowed each man individually to plant corn for his own household and to trust to themselves for that. In all other things they went on in the general way as before.

So every family was assigned a parcel of land, according to the proportion of their number, with that in view—all boys and children being included under some family. This was very successful. It made all hands very industrious, so that much more corn was planted than otherwise would have been by any means the governor or any other could devise, and saved him a great deal of trouble, and gave far better satisfaction. The women now went willingly into the field, and took their little ones with them to plant corn, while before they complained of weakness and inability.

The failure of this experiment of communal service, which was tried for several years by good and honest men, proves the emptiness of the theory of Plato and other ancients, which has been applauded by some of later times. They said that the removal of private property and the possession of all things in common in a community would make a state happy and flourishing—as if they were wiser than God!

For, in our instance, community of property was found to breed much confusion and discontent, and greatly hindered employment which would have been to the general benefit and comfort of all. This happened because the young men, who were most able and fit for service, objected to being forced to spend their time and strength in working for other men's wives and children without any recompense. The strong man or the resourceful man had no more share of food or clothes than the weak man who was not able to do a quarter of the work that the other could. This was thought injustice. The aged and graver men, who were ranked and equalized in labor, food, and clothes with the humbler and younger ones, thought it some indignity and disrespect to them. As for the men's wives who were obliged to do service for other men (such as cooking, washing their clothes, etc.), they considered it a kind of slavery, and many husbands would not allow it.

If (it was thought) all were to share alike and all were

to do alike, then all were on an equality throughout, and one was as good as another. And so, if it did not actually abolish those very relations which God himself has set among men, it did at least greatly diminish the mutual respect that is so important to be preserved among them. Let none argue that the failure of this experiment is due to human failing rather than to this communistic plan of life in itself. I answer that, since all men have this failing in them, this is the very reason why God in His wisdom saw that another plan of life other than communism was more suitable for them.

But to return. After this had been settled and our corn was planted in this way, all our food supplies were consumed and we had to rely on God's providence, often at night not knowing where to get a bit of anything next day. And so, as one person truly noted, we had need above all people in the world to pray to God and ask Him to give us our daily bread.

In the month of July the ship called the *Anne* arrived, of which Mr. William Pierce was captain, and about a week or ten days later came the pinnace (a small ship) which they had lost in foul weather at sea, a fine new vessel of about forty-four tons, which the company had built to stay in the country. They brought about sixty settlers for the colony, some of them very useful persons who became good members to the body, and some were the wives and children of those who were here already. But some of the new settlers were so unruly that we were obliged to go to the expense of sending them home again the next year.

The passengers, when they saw the poor condition of those ashore, were much daunted and dismayed and, according to their different characters, responded differently. Some wished themselves in England again; others began weeping, imagining what their own misery would be from what they saw before them. Others pitied the distress they saw their friends had been in so long and still were under. In a word, all were full of sadness.

Some few of our old friends rejoiced to see us again and

to know that it was no worse with us, for they could not expect it to be better. And they hoped that now we would enjoy better days together. And it was certainly not unnatural that the new arrivals should be thus affected, for we settlers were in a very poor condition. Many of us were ragged in clothing, and some little better than half-naked, though some few who were well stocked before were well-enough clothed.

But, as for food, we were all alike. The best dish we could present to our friends was a lobster or a piece of fish, without any bread or anything else but a cup of fair spring water. The long continuance of this diet, and our labors, had somewhat dimmed the freshness of our complexions. But God gave us health and strength and showed us by experience the truth of that word: "Man liveth not by bread alone, but by every word that proceedeth out of the mouth of the Lord doth a man live" (Deut. 8:3).

When I think how sadly the Scripture speaks of the famine in Jacob's time when he said to his sons, "Go buy us food, that we may live and not die," and that the famine was great in the land and yet they had such great herds of cattle of various kinds, which besides meat produce other foods such as milk, butter, and cheese, and yet this was considered a sore affliction—when we think of this, then we see that the affliction of these settlers must have been very great, who not only lacked the staff of life, but all these things, and had no Egypt to go to. But God fed us out of the sea for the most part, so wonderful is His providence over His own in all ages! For His mercy endureth for ever.

Now the original settlers were afraid that their corn, when it was ripe, would have to be shared with the newcomers, and that the provisions which the latter had brought with them would give out before the year was over—as indeed they did. So they went to the governor and begged him that, since he had agreed to allow them to plant their corn for their own use, and accordingly they had taken extraordinary pains about it, they might be permitted to keep it. They would rather do that

than have a bit of the food just come in the ship. They were content to wait till harvest for their own and let the newcomers enjoy what they had brought. Their request was granted them, and it satisfied both sides, for the newcomers were afraid that the hungry settlers would eat up the provisions they had brought and that they themselves would then fall into a similar condition of famine.

The ship was loaded in a short time with clapboard, by the help of many hands. We also sent in her all the beaver and other furs we had, and Mr. Winslow was sent over with her to provide information to the company in England and to procure such things as were required.

Harvest time had now come, and then, instead of famine, God gave us plenty, and the face of things was changed, to the rejoicing of the hearts of many, for which we blessed God. And the effect of our planting by private ownership was clearly seen, for all had enough to last the year through, and some of the abler sort and more industrious had enough and sufficient to spare and sell to others. In fact, no general want or famine has been among us since, to this day.

CHAPTER ELEVEN

Death of a Pastor

The time for the election of the officers for the year having come and the number of people having increased and the business of government accordingly, I requested them to change the officials and give me more assistants for my help and advice. I pointed out that, if it was an honor or advantage to be placed in authority, it was only right that others should share in the honor. Also, if it was a burden (as it certainly was!), it was only fair that others should help to bear it—and that this, in fact, was the purpose of the annual elections.

The outcome was that, though before there had been only one assistant, they now chose five (giving the governor a double vote), and afterwards increased them to seven. This plan has been continued to this day.

Having at some trouble and expense new-masted and rigged our pinnace, in the beginning of March, 1624, we sent her well-supplied to the eastward, fishing. She arrived safely at a place called Damariscove, and was well-harbored where ships were accustomed to anchor, with some other ships from England, already there. But shortly after there arose such a violent and extraordinary storm that the seas broke into the harbor in a way that had never been known before, and drove her against great rocks, which beat such a hole in her side that a horse and cart might have been driven through, and then she drifted into deep water, where she lay sunk. The captain was drowned, but the rest of the men, except one, with difficulty saved their lives. All her provisions, salt, etc., were lost. Here she lay for some time.

But, when some of the fishing-boats' captains heard what had happened, they said it was a pity that so fine a vessel should be lost, and sent us word that if we would bear the expense, they would show us how to float her, and let us have their carpenters to mend her. We thanked them and sent men for the purpose, and beaver skins to cover the cost of labor and repairs. So they got coopers to trim I know not how many tons of casks. And, having made them tight and fastened them to her at low water, they buoyed her up and hauled her ashore with many hands in a convenient place where she could be worked on. Then they set several carpenters to work at her, and others to saw planks, and at last fitted her out and got her home. But it cost a great deal of money to recover her and to buy rigging and sails for her, both now and when she lost her mast before. So she proved an expensive vessel to the poor plantation.

In 1625 Captain Standish returned to England to settle some matters relating to the colony and to speak with our friends there. He returned in April of 1626. He received a warm welcome, but the news he brought was sad in many regards, not only as to the losses which our friends had suffered, but also the tidings that Mr. John Robinson, our old pastor, was dead, which saddened us much, and not without good reason. Our adversaries had long been plotting to hinder his coming here, but the Lord had appointed him a better place.

An account of his death is given in these few lines written to the Governor and Mr. Brewster:

> *Roger White at Leyden to Governor Bradford*
> *and William Brewster at New Plymouth*
> Loving and kind Friends,
> I do not know whether this will ever come to your hands, or miscarry as my other letters have done. But, because of the Lord's dealing with us here, I have had a great wish to

write to you, knowing your desire to participate with us both in our joys and sorrows, as we do with you. This is to give you to understand that it has pleased the Lord to take out of this vale of tears your and our loving and faithful pastor, and my dear and reverend brother, Mr. John Robinson, who was ill for some eight days. He began to sicken on Saturday morning. Yet the next day (being the Lord's Day) he taught us twice. The week after he grew daily weaker, but was without pain. The medicine he took seemed to benefit him, but he grew weaker every day, though he remained sensible to the last. He fell sick on February 22nd and departed this life on March 1st.

During his illness all his friends came to see him. If either prayers or tears or care could have saved his life, he would never have departed from here. But he, having faithfully finished his course and performed the work which the Lord had appointed him here to do, now rests with the Lord in eternal happiness.

Since his going our Church lacks a governor, yet we still continue by the mercy of God, and hold close together in peace and quietness. And we so hope to continue to do, though we are very weak. We wish (if such were the will of God) that you and we were again united, either there or here. But, seeing it is the will of the Lord thus to dispose of things, we must labor with patience to rest contented till it please the Lord to do otherwise.

As for news, there is not much. In England we have lost our old King James, who departed this life about a month ago; and here in the Netherlands they have lost the old prince, Grave Maurice, both having departed this life since my brother Robinson.

Thus with my love remembered, I take leave and rest,
Your assured loving friend,
Roger White
Leyden, April 28th, 1625

Thus these two great princes and the colonists' old pastor left this world about the same time. Death makes no difference.

Our other friends from Leyden wrote many sad letters to us, lamenting the heavy loss of their pastor. And, though they would gladly have come to us, they saw no probability of it, but concluded that all their hopes were at an end. And besides, many, being aged, began to drop away by death.

We were greatly perplexed—and not without cause. But we took courage, and the Lord so helped us, whose work we had in hand, that now when we seemed at the lowest ebb we began to rise again. And, being stripped as it were of all human helps and props, by His divine providence we were not only upheld and sustained, but our example was both honored and imitated by others.

Having now no fishing business or other things to attend to besides our trading and planting, we set ourselves to follow these with the greatest diligence we could. When the settlers discovered that our spare corn was a commodity worth six shillings a bushel, they spared no pains in planting it. The governor and those appointed to manage the trade with the Indians (for it was still retained for the general benefit, and none were allowed to trade for themselves) cooperated. So, lacking goods to trade with, and hearing that a settlement which had existed at Monhegan was ending and many useful goods were to be sold, I and Mr. Winslow took a boat and some hands and went there. We also bought some goats, which we distributed among the colonists as they thought fit in exchange for corn.

By this means we were well-furnished with articles for trading, and were able to repay some of our previous debts, such as the money raised by Captain Standish and the balance of former debts. With these goods and our corn (when harvested), we traded profitably, and were able to meet our engagements punctually, and get some clothing for the people, and still had some supplies in hand. But soon we began to be envied by others, who went and supplied the Indians with corn and beat down the price, giving them twice as much as we had done, and under-traded us with other articles, too.

This year we sent Mr. Allerton to England, and gave him instructions to settle our debts with the men there on as good terms as he could, for which composition Captain Standish had paved the way the year before. We ordered him not to conclude anything permanently until we knew the terms and had well considered them, but to instead arrange preliminaries as well as he could, and refer the conclusion to us. We also gave him commission under our hands and seals to raise some money, provided it did not exceed the sum specified, for which we pledged ourselves, and instructed him how to spend it for the use of the plantation.

Finding that we ran great risks in taking such long voyages in a small open boat, especially during the winter, we began to think how we could get a small pinnace. It was even more necessary since others were paying the Indians half as much corn again as we had formerly given, and in such a small boat as we currently had we could not carry a quantity sufficient for our purposes. We had no ship-builder among us, nor did we know how to get one at present. But we had a resourceful man who was a house carpenter, who had worked under the ship-builder when he was building our boats. So, at our request, he tried his skill, and took one of the biggest of our shallops, sawed her across the middle, lengthened her about five or six feet, strengthened her with timbers, built her up, decked her, and made her into a convenient and serviceable vessel suitable for our use. We got her finished and fitted with sails and anchors for the coming year, and she did us service for seven years.

CHAPTER TWELVE

Friends from Leyden

Before we sent Mr. Allerton to England this year, I and some of the main members of the plantation seriously considered how best to obtain payment for the many debts which lay so heavily upon us, and also how, if possible, to bring over some of our friends at Leyden, who wished so much to come to us and whose company we equally desired. To effect this, the leading men of the colony resolved upon a daring course, not knowing how to accomplish their objects otherwise. This was, that we would purchase the trade of the settlement (now owned jointly by the settlers, as a body, and by the adventurers) for a certain period, and in that time to undertake to pay the £1800 and all the rest of the debts that the plantation then owed, which amounted to about £600 more. Then the trade of the settlement would revert to common ownership at the end of the period.

    Mr. Allerton took a copy of this agreement to England, and had orders to arrange to bring over some of our friends from Leyden, if possible, and to tell them that if any of them would join with us we would thankfully accept their partnership.

    Mr. Allerton settled everything satisfactorily in England and returned to the colony in the early spring of 1628 with our supplies for trading. He also brought a fair stock of goods for the settlement and an account of the beaver skins sold and of the money expended for goods and the payment of other debts.

Mr. Allerton also brought us word that a reasonable number of the congregation at Leyden would be sent over next year without fail, if the Lord pleased to bless their journey.

The next year, in 1629, Mr. Allerton returned to England. That same year he sent over some of the congregation remaining in Leyden. They took passage on ships that came to Salem, which brought over many godly persons to begin the settlements and churches of Christ there and in the Bay of Massachusetts. So their friends here were rewarded for our long delay with double blessing in that we not only enjoyed them now, when so recently all our hopes had seemed to be blasted, but with them came other godly friends and Christian brethren, to plant a still larger harvest to the Lord for the increase of His churches and people in these parts.

It was to the astonishment of many and almost to the wonder of the world that from so small a beginning such great things should result—as in due time was revealed—and that there should be a resting place for so many of the Lord's people here when so sharp a scourge had come upon their own nation. But it was the Lord's doing, and it ought to be marvelous in our eyes.

Though we rejoiced to have the company of our brethren, their arrival brought great expense and labor to the colonists already here. Their friends here had to provide corn and other provisions for them till they could reap a crop, which was some time. The newcomers had to be maintained upwards of 16 to 18 months, during which time all they could do was to build houses and prepare land for planting next season, for the season was too far spent for planting when they arrived.

The expenses of supporting them all this time was a very great sum. I make special note of this for various reasons: first, to show a rare example of brotherly love and Christian care in fulfilling our promises to our brethren. Secondly, to prove that there was more than the work of man in these achievements—for to have successfully persuaded such able friends to join us in the enterprise, and then to stand by them so faithfully in the face of such risks, most of us never having seen their faces to this day, must certainly be the special work of God. I cannot help but wonder at His ways and works towards His servants, and humbly desire to bless His holy name for His great mercies granted us thus far.

In 1630 John Billington the elder, one of those who came over with us in the beginning, was arraigned, and both by grand and petty jury found guilty of willful murder by plain and notorious evidence, and was accordingly executed.

This, the first execution among us, was a great sadness to us. We took all possible pains in the trial, and consulted Mr. Winthrop and the other leading men at the Bay of Massachusetts recently arrived, who concurred with us that he ought to die and the land be purged of blood. He and some of his relatives had often been punished for misconduct before, for he was from one of the profanest families among us. They came from London, and I know not by what influence they were shuffled into the first body of settlers. The charge against him was that he waylaid a young man, one John Newcomin, about a former quarrel, and shot him with a gun, by which he died.

It pleased the Lord to visit us in 1633 with an infectious fever of which many fell very ill, and upwards of twenty persons died—men, women and children, and several of our oldest friends who had lived in Holland. Among them were Thomas Blossom, Richard Masterson, and some others. And, in the end, after he had helped others much, Samuel Fuller our physician died, who had been a great help and comfort to us not only in his profession but also as a deacon of the church, a godly man, always ready to serve his fellows. He was much missed after his death, and he and the rest of our brethren who died were much lamented by us. This brought much sadness and mourning among us and caused us to humble ourselves and seek the Lord.

Towards winter it pleased the Lord that the sickness ceased. This disease also swept away many of the Indians from the adjoining parts.

The spring before, especially the month of May, there had been a quantity of a great sort of fly as large as wasps or bumblebees, which came out of holes in the ground, filling all the woods and eating the crops and undergrowth in the forests. They made such a constant yelling noise that the woods rang with them, till they were ready to deafen the hearers. They have not been heard or seen before or since by the English. The Indians told us that sickness would follow these creatures, and so it did, in June, July, and August, during the greatest heat of the summer.

It pleased the Lord to enable us this year to send home a great quantity of beaver skins, besides paying all our expenses and debts here in the country, which was a great encouragement to our friends in England.

CHAPTER THIRTEEN

A Murder Trial

In 1638 Mr. Thomas Prince was chosen governor.
Among other enormities that occurred this same year, three men were tried and executed for robbery and murder. Their names were Arthur Peach, Thomas Jackson, and Richard Stinnings. There was a fourth, Daniel Crose, who was also found guilty, but he escaped and could not be found. Arthur Peach was the ringleader. He was a strong and desperate young man and had been one of the soldiers in the Pequot war. He had done as good a service as any there, always being one of the first in any attack. But, being now out of employment and reluctant to work, and taking to idle ways and company, he intended to go to the Dutch colony, and had lured the other three, who were servants and apprentices, to go with him.

But there was also another cause for his going away secretly in this way, which was the fact that he had not only run into debt but had seduced a girl, a maid-servant in the town, and fear of punishment made him wish to get away, though this was not known till after his death.

The other three men ran away from their masters in the night and could not be found, for they didn't go by the ordinary route but shaped such a course as they thought would evade pursuit. Finding themselves somewhere between the Bay of Massachusetts and the Narragansetts' country, and wishing to rest, they made a fire a little off the road by the wayside, and took tobacco.

At length there came a Narragansett Indian by, who had been trading at the Bay and had some cloth and beads with him. They had met him the day before, and now he was returning. Peach called him to come and drink tobacco with them, and he came and sat down. Peach had previously told the others he would kill the Indian and take his goods. The others were afraid, but Peach said, "Hang the rogue; he has killed many of us." So they let him do as he wanted, and when he saw his opportunity he took his rapier and ran the man through the body once or twice, and took from him five fathoms of wampum and three coats of cloth. Then they went their way, leaving him for dead.

But the Indian managed to scramble up when they had gone and make his way home. By this means they were discovered, and the Indians caught them. For, needing a canoe to take them over the water and not thinking their act was known, they asked the Indians to help them. After they were caught they were taken to Aquidnett Island by the sachem's command and were there accused of the deed and examined and arrested by the English.

The Indians sent for Mr. Williams and made grievous complaint, and the friends and relatives of the injured native were ready to rise up in arms and incite the rest to do the same, believing they would now find the Pequot's words were true, which was that the English would turn upon them and kill them all. But Mr. Williams quieted them and told them that they would see justice done on the offenders. Then he went to the wounded man and took Mr. James, the physician, with him.

The Indian told him who had done it and how it was done. The physician found the Indian's wounds mortal and said that he could not possibly live, as he testified upon oath before the jury in open court. He died shortly after.

The governor at the Bay was made aware of it, but referred it to New Plymouth because the act was committed in our jurisdiction, but he urged that by all means justice should be done or else it would cause a war. (Despite this, some of the more ignorant colonists objected and said that an Englishman should not be put to death for an Indian.)

So at last the murderers were brought home from the Island. And, after being tried and the evidence produced, they all in the end freely confessed to all the Indian had accused them of, and admitted that they had done it in the way described. So they were condemned by the jury and executed.

Some of the Narragansett Indians and the murdered man's friends were present for the execution, which showed them that justice had been rendered. But it was a matter of much sadness to us here, for this was the second execution since we came—both being for willful murder.

It pleased God about this time to bless the country with such an influx of people that it was much enriched, and cattle of all kinds stood at high prices for many years. Cows were sold at £20, some at £25 apiece, sometimes even at £28. A cow-calf usually fetched £10; a milk goat £3, and sometimes £4; and she-kids thirty shillings and often £2 apiece. By this means the original settlers who had stock began to increase in wealth. Corn also commanded a high price, at six shillings a bushel.

This year, about the 1st or 2nd of June, we had a fearful earthquake. Here it was heard before it was felt. It began with a rumbling noise, or low murmur, like remote thunder. It came from the northward and passed southward. As the noise approached the earth began to shake, and at length it did so with such violence that platters, dishes, and other things standing on shelves came clattering down, and people were afraid for the houses themselves.

It was very terrible for a while, and as the men sat talking in the house, some women and others were just out of doors, and the earth shook with such violence that they could not remain standing without catching hold of the posts and palings near by. But the violence did not last long. About half an hour after, or less, came another noise and shaking, but not

as severe as previously and not lasting long.

Some ships along the coast were shaken by it, but it was not only felt near the sea, for the Indians noticed it inland. So powerful is the mighty hand of the Lord as to make both the earth and the sea to shake and the mountains to tremble before Him when He pleases, and who can stay His hand?

It was observed that the summers for several years after this earthquake were not as hot and seasonable for the ripening of corn and other fruits as formerly, but were colder and more moist and subject to early and ill-timed frosts, so that often much Indian corn failed. Whether this was the cause, I leave it to naturalists to judge.

CHAPTER FOURTEEN

His Mercy Endures Forever

I must now relate an event which brought great sadness and mourning to us all. About the 18th of April, 1643, our reverend elder, my dear and loving friend, Mr. William Brewster, died. He was a man who had done and suffered much for the Lord Jesus and the gospel's sake, and had borne his part in weal or woe with this poor persecuted church for over thirty-five years in England, Holland, and this wilderness, and had done both the Lord and us faithful service in his calling.

Despite the many troubles and sorrows he passed through, the Lord upheld him to a great age. He was nearly eighty years old, if not quite, when he died. In the end the Lord added one final blessing besides all the rest, which is that he died in his bed in peace, in the midst of his friends, who mourned and wept over him and who gave him what help and comfort they could. And he, too, comforted them while he could.

His illness was not long, and until the last day he remained able to move about. His speech continued until about the last half-day, and then failed him; and at about 9 or 10 o'clock that evening he died, without any pangs at all. A few hours earlier he drew his breath short, and some few minutes from the end he drew it long, like a man fallen into a sound sleep—and thus he sweetly departed this life into a better.

I would ask, was he the worse for any of his former sufferings? What do I say? Worse? No, he was surely the better, for now they were added to his honor. "It is a manifest token," says the apostle, "of the righteous judgment of God that ye may be counted worthy of the Kingdom of God, for which ye also suffer; seeing it is a righteous thing with God to recompense tribulation to them that trouble you: and to you who are troubled, rest with us, when the Lord Jesus shall be revealed from Heaven, with His mighty angels" (2 Thess. 1:5-7). And Peter tells us: "If you be reproached for the name of Christ, happy are ye, for the spirit of glory and of God resteth upon you" (1 Pet. 4:14).

What does it matter that he lacked the riches and pleasures of the world in this life and pompous monuments at his funeral? Yet "the memory of the just shall be blessed, when the name of the wicked shall rot" along with their marble monuments (Prov. 10:7).

I must say at least something of his life. After he had attained some learning (the knowledge of the Latin tongue and some insight into Greek) and had spent some little time at Cambridge—then being first seasoned with the seeds of grace and virtue—he went to court and served that religious and godly gentleman, Mr. Davison, for several years, when he was Secretary of State. His master found him so discreet and faithful that he trusted him more than all the others who were round him, and employed him in all matters of greatest trust and secrecy. He considered him rather as a son than a servant. And, knowing his wisdom and godliness, he would converse with him in private more as a friend and equal than as a master.

Afterwards Mr. Brewster went and lived in the country, much respected by his friends and the gentlemen of the neighborhood, especially the godly and religious. He did much good there by promoting and furthering religion, not only by his practice and example and the encouragement of others, but by procuring good preachers for the places thereabouts and persuading others to help and assist in such work, generally taking most of the expense on himself—

sometimes even beyond his means.

Thus he continued for many years, doing the best he could and walking according to the light he saw, till the Lord revealed Himself further to him. In the end, the tyranny of the bishops against godly preachers and people, in silencing the former and persecuting the latter, caused him and many more to look further into things and to realize the unlawfulness of their episcopal callings and to feel the burden of their many antichristian corruptions, which both he and they attempted to throw off. In this they succeeded, as the beginning of this volume shows.

After we had joined ourselves together in communion (as was mentioned earlier), he was a special help and support to us. On the Lord's Day we generally met at his house, which was a manor of the bishop's, and he entertained us with great kindness when we came, providing for us at heavy expense to himself. He was the leader of those who were captured at Boston in Lincolnshire, suffering the greatest loss, and was one of the seven who were kept longest in prison and afterwards bound over to the assizes.

After he came to Holland he suffered much hardship, having spent most of his wealth, with a large family to support, and being from his upbringing and previous mode of life not so fit for such laborious employment as others were. But he always bore his troubles with much cheerfulness and contentment.

Towards the latter part of those twelve years spent in Holland his circumstances improved, and he lived well and plentifully. For through his knowledge of Latin he was able to teach many foreign students English. By his method they acquired it quickly and with great fluency, for he drew up rules to learn it by, after the manner of teaching Latin. And many gentlemen, both Danes and Germans, came to him, some of them being sons of distinguished men. By the help of some friends he was also able to set up a printing press, and thus had employment enough. And, since many books were forbidden to be printed in England, they might have had more work than they could do.

But, on moving to this country, all these things were laid aside again and a new way of living must be framed, in which he was in no way unwilling to take his part and bear his burden with the rest, living often for many months without corn or bread, with nothing but fish to eat, and often not even that. He drank nothing but water for many years—indeed until five or six years before his death—and yet by the blessing of God he lived in health to a very old age. He labored in the fields as long as he was able. Yet, when the church had no other minister, he taught twice every Sabbath, and did so both powerfully and profitably, to the great edification and comfort of his hearers, many being brought to God by his ministry. He did more in this way in a single year than many who have their hundreds a year do in all their lives.

As for his personal qualities, he was blessed far beyond many. He was wise and discreet and well-spoken, having a grave and deliberate utterance, with a very cheerful spirit. He was very sociable and pleasant among his friends, of a humble and modest mind and a peaceable disposition, under-valuing himself and his own abilities and sometimes over-valuing others. He was innocent in his life and conversation, which gained him the love of those without as well as those within the church. Nevertheless he would tell people plainly of their faults, both publicly and privately, but in such a way that it was usually well taken.

He was tender-hearted and compassionate with those in misery, especially when they were of good birth and rank and had fallen into want and poverty either for religion's sake or through the oppression of others; he would always say that of all men such deserved to be most pitied. No one displeased him more than those who would haughtily and proudly exalt themselves, having risen from nothing and having little else to commend them than a few fine clothes or more possessions than others.

When preaching, he deeply moved and stirred the emotions, and he was very plain and direct in what he taught, being thereby the more profitable to his hearers. He had a singularly good gift of prayer, both public and private, in opening the heart and conscience before God, in the humble confession of sin, and begging the mercies of God in Christ for the pardon of it. He always thought it better for ministers to pray oftener and divide their prayers rather than to be long and tedious.

In the government of the church (which was proper to his office as elder), he was careful to preserve good order and purity both in doctrine and communion, and to suppress any error or contention that might begin to arise. And God accordingly gave success to his endeavors in this all his days, and he was permitted to see the fruit of his labors.

But I end, even though I have only mentioned a few things briefly.

I must here pause and wonder at the marvelous providence of God that, despite the many changes our people went through and the many enemies we had and the difficulties we met with, so many of us should live to very old age. It was not only our reverend elder, but many more of us, some dying about and before this time, and some still living, who reached sixty or sixty-five years of age, others seventy and over, and some nearly eighty, as he was.

This must be explained by other than natural reasons, for it is found in experience that change of air, hunger, unwholesome food, much drinking of water, sorrows and troubles, etc., are all enemies to health, causing many diseases, loss of natural vigor, and shortness of life. Yet all those unfavorable conditions were our lot.

We went from England to Holland, where we found both worse air and food than where we came from. Then, after enduring a long imprisonment, as it were, aboard ship, we came to New England, and our way of living here has already been shown, as well as what trials, troubles, fears, wants, and sorrows we were exposed to. In a sense we may say with the apostle that we were "in journeyings often, in perils of water, in perils of robbers, in perils by our own nation, in perils by the heathen, in perils in the wilderness, in perils on the sea, in perils among false brethren; in weariness and painfulness, in watchings often, in hunger and thirst, in fastings often, in cold and nakedness" (2 Cor. 11:26-27).

What was it then that upheld us? It was God's presence and mercy that preserved our spirits: "Thou hast granted me life and favour, and Thy visitation hath preserved my spirit" (Job 10:12). He that upheld the apostle upheld us. We were "persecuted, but not forsaken; cast down, but not destroyed" (2 Cor. 4:9). We were "as unknown, and yet well known; as dying, and behold we live; as chastened, and not killed" (2 Cor. 6:9).

God, it seems, desired all men to behold and observe such mercies and works of His providence towards His people so that they in like cases might be encouraged to depend upon God in their trials and also bless His name when they see His goodness towards others. Man lives not by bread alone.

It is not by good and dainty food, by peace and rest and heart's ease, in enjoying the contentment and good things of this world only, that health is preserved and life prolonged. God in such examples desires the world to see and behold that He can do it without them. And if the world will shut its eyes and take no notice of it, yet He desires His people to see and consider it.

Daniel was better off with vegetables than others were with the king's luxuries. Jacob, though he went from his own nation to another people and passed through famine, fear, and many afflictions, yet lived till old age and died sweetly, and rested in the Lord, as countless others of God's servants have done and still shall do through God's goodness, despite all the malice of their enemies, for "the branch of the wicked shall be cut off before his day" and "bloody and deceitful men shall not live out half their days" (Job 15:32; Psa. 55:23).

APPENDIX

Letter of Pastor John Robinson

Mr. John Robinson in Holland to the Pilgrims departing from Southampton for New England:

Loving Christian Friends,

I salute you all heartily in the Lord, for in my best affections and most earnest longings I am present with you even though I am forced for a time to be bodily absent from you. I say forced, for God knows how willingly—and with how much desire—I would have borne my part with you in this first hardship and burden, if I weren't held back for the present by dire necessity. Think of me in the meantime as of a man cut in half, with great pain, and (physical limitations set aside) as having his better part with you. I'm certain that in your godly wisdom you can foresee what is necessary for your present situation, yet I thought it my duty to add some further encouragement to spur you on, even to those who run already—not because you need it, but because I owe it to you out of love and duty.

First, just as we ought to daily renew our repentance with our God especially for our known sins (as well as for our unknown sins), so on such an occasion of difficulty and danger as lies before you the Lord also calls us in a particular way both to more closely examine ourselves and carefully reform our ways in His sight, lest He remember our sins which have been forgotten by us or are unrepented of, and lest, as a judgment upon us, He leave us to be swallowed up in one danger or another.

But, on the other hand, when sin has been taken away by earnest repentance, and when the Lord's pardon is sealed up into our conscience by His Spirit, our security and peace in all dangers will be great indeed, and our comfort in all our distresses will be sweet, with happy deliverance from all evil, whether in life or in death.

Now, after this heavenly peace with God and our own conscience, we must diligently provide for peace with all men as far as we are able, especially with our brethren. To accomplish this we must be careful that we ourselves neither give nor easily take offense. "Woe be unto the world for offenses; for though it be necessary (considering the malice of Satan and man's corruption) that offenses come, yet woe unto the man or woman either, by whom the offense comes," says Christ (see Matt. 18:7). And, if offenses arising from thoughtless actions innocent in themselves are more to be feared than death itself—as the apostle teaches (1 Cor. 9:15)—how much more should we fear those which arise from evil, in which neither the honor of God nor a love for man has even been considered.

Nor is it enough for us to simply keep ourselves (by the grace of God) from giving offense, but we must also be armed against taking offense when it is given by others. For, if we lack the love that covers a multitude of offenses or sins, as the Scripture says, the work of grace within us is very incomplete. Neither are you exhorted to this grace only upon the common grounds of Christianity. Persons ready to take offense either lack the love which should cover offenses; or the wisdom to properly consider human weakness; or lastly, are great though secret hypocrites, as Christ our Lord teaches (Matt. 7:1-3). In my own experience I have found few who are quicker to give offense than those who easily take it. Those who allow themselves to be easily offended have never become beneficial and profitable members in societies.

But there are, besides, many reasons why you above others should take special care in this matter. Many of you are strangers to each other and to each other's weaknesses. Therefore you have much greater need to be on guard lest, when something unsuspected appears in someone, you become disturbed by it beyond reason. This requires much wisdom and love at your hands.

Further, the plans for your intended civil community will offer continual opportunities for offense, and will be like fuel to the fire unless you diligently quench it with brotherly patience and forbearance. And, if taking offense needlessly or easily at another person should be so carefully avoided, how much more should we beware of taking offense at God himself—which we do as often as we complain about His providence in our trials, or bear impatiently such afflictions as He pleases to visit upon us! Store up, therefore, patience against the evil day when we will be tempted to take offense at the Lord Himself in His holy and just works.

A fourth thing you must carefully watch for concerns your occupations and employments. These will be common to all, and you must always strive for the general good of all and avoid like a plague any selfish thoughts or inclinations. You must never withhold your hand from labor because you are thinking of yourself instead of others. Let each of you suppress within yourself any private prejudice or bias, and treat such thoughts like rebels that war against the common good.

And, just like we are careful not to have a new house shaken with any violence before it is well settled and before the walls and roof are put on, so you also, brethren, must be even more diligent to see that the house of God, which you are and are to be, be not shaken with unnecessary novelties or other oppositions when it is first being built.

Lastly, since you are to become a civil body and will be administering among yourselves a civil government, and since you are supplied with ordinary persons from whom you will elect someone to the office of government, let your wisdom and godliness appear not only in choosing such persons as will entirely love and promote the common good, but also in yielding them all due honor and obedience in their lawful administrations. You must not consider them according to the nature of their person, but must consider God's ordinance for your good, and recognize that He has appointed them. So also you must not be like the foolish multitude who honors a man with fancy clothes more than either the virtuous mind of the wearer or the glorious ordinance of the Lord. But you know better, and understand that the image of the Lord's power and authority which the magistrate bears is honorable, no matter how lowly the person may be. And this duty you can the more willingly perform because you are at present to have only those for your governors as you yourselves shall choose.

Several other things of importance I could remind you of, but I know you are not heedless of these things, for there are many among you who are quite well able both to admonish themselves and others. These few things, therefore, I do earnestly commend to your consideration and conscience, and join to them my daily incessant prayers unto the Lord, asking Him who made the heavens and the earth, the sea and all rivers of waters, and whose providence is over all His works—especially over all His dear children for good—to so guide and guard you in your ways, both inwardly by His Spirit and outwardly by the hand of His power, that both you and we also may praise His name all the days of our lives. Fare you well in Him in whom you trust and in whom I rest.

An unfeigned well-willer of your happy success in this hopeful voyage,

JOHN ROBINSON

Made in the
USA
Monee, IL